The Dragon Balloon

Written by Cheryl Palin

Illustrated by Sarah Jennings

OXFORD

UNIVERSITY PRESS

OXFORD
UNIVERSITY PRESS

Great Clarendon Street, Oxford, OX2 6DP, United Kingdom

Oxford University Press is a department of the University
of Oxford. It furthers the University's objective of excellence
in research, scholarship, and education by publishing
worldwide. Oxford is a registered trade mark of Oxford
University Press in the UK and in certain other countries

Text © Cheryl Palin 2017
Illustrations © Sarah Jennings 2017
Inside cover notes written by Liz Miles

The moral rights of the author have been asserted

First published 2017

British Library Cataloguing in Publication Data
Data available

ISBN: 978-0-19-841483-4

10 9 8 7 6 5

Paper used in the production of this book is a natural, recyclable product
made from wood grown in sustainable forests. The manufacturing process
conforms to the environmental regulations of the country of origin.

Printed in China

Acknowledgements

Series Editor: Nikki Gamble

Pip has a balloon.

A big dragon balloon!

5

The balloon bobs up and up.

Can Tom grab it?

Can Ben grab it?

It is fun!

Get it in the net!

A hen has to run.

Dad picks Pip up.